YOUR KNOWLEDGE HAS VALUE

Hülya Akkaş

Analysis of Woody Allen's short story "Sam you made the pants too fragrant"

GRIN Verlag

Bibliografische Information der Deutschen Nationalbibliothek:

Die Deutsche Bibliothek verzeichnet diese Publikation in der Deutschen National-
bibliografie; detaillierte bibliografische Daten sind im Internet über http://dnb.d-
nb.de/ abrufbar.

Imprint:

Copyright © 2008 GRIN Verlag GmbH
Druck und Bindung: Books on Demand GmbH, Norderstedt Germany
ISBN: 978-3-640-56441-5

This book at GRIN:

http://www.grin.com/en/e-book/145460/analysis-of-woody-allen-s-short-story-sam-
you-made-the-pants-too-fragrant

Seminar: Mere Anarchy? The Films and Short Stories of Woody Allen
FB 3 Sprach-, Literatur- und Medienwissenschaften

Semester: SoSe 2008

"Sam, You Made the Pants Too Fragrant"
Woody Allen and progress in life
(The Pitfalls of Progress)

Akkaş, Hülya
MA-LCM (Comparative Studies), 2
2008-07-30

OUTLINE

Introduction   3

1. "Sam, you made the pants too fragrant"   5

    1.1 The story   5

        1.1.1 A summary of the plot   5

        1.1.2 A possible background of the story   7

    1.2 Analyzing the story   8

2. Conclusion: Woody Allen and progress in life   11

3. Bibliography   14

Introduction

Woody Allen, born Allen Stewart Konigsberg[1], is a Jewish artist, who is mostly known as filmmaker – but he carries several faces and puts his work into several fields. Although his movies often seem to deal with the same topics, Allen never concentrates on only one genre, as we worked out during our seminar and the expert sessions. Besides his widely spread image of the intellectual and humorous filmmaker, he put his thoughts into prose and stand-up comedy, too; he wrote articles for magazines like *New York Times, Playboy* or *The New Republic*[2] and of course he is known through his roles in his own films. By acting out his own roles he has written, Woody Allen as the private person and the public known Woody Allen, somehow melted together; so, the viewer can find more personal elements in Allen`s movies, as he or she may expect. Or better said, he by some means performed himself through the stories of his films.

Besides the fact that Allen mostly acted out the role of the protagonist in his movies and barring that the topics of the movies seem to be repetitive, there are other typical elements that continuously appear in his movies, what in this paper – as it already have been in our expert session – will be depicted as "allenesque elements". These are for instance the neurotic characters, the Jewishness (that apparently refers to his private persona), the psycho-analysis, the fusion of reality and fiction, unhappy relationships, love-affairs and the element of the anxious behavior, towards special issues, of some of his characters are just a number of the main subjects that are typical of Woody Allen stories. But Allen`s audience is not only "confronted" with these topics in his movies; as already mentioned, he also developed his ideas in prose and short stories.

With his book "Mere Anarchy", in 2007 Woody Allen brought out his fourth collection of short stories and the first since 27 years. During this time he was mostly occupied with his movies; nearly every year, a new Allen movie was released. His new short story collection "Mere Anarchy" contains 18 pieces of which ten have been published in the *New Yorker*.[3] Furthermore the reader can encounter the well known and already mentioned "allenesque"

---

[1] Comp.: FUCHS, Wolfgang J.: Die vielen Gesichter des Woody Allen. Köln: Benedikt Taschen Verlag, 1986, p. 7.
[2] Comp.: YACOWAR, Maurice: Loser Take All. The Comic Art of Woody Allen. USA: Frederick Ungar Publishing Co., Inc., 1979, p. 73.
[3] Comp.:https://www.commentarymagazine.com/viewarticle.cfm/mere-anarchy-by-woody-allen-10944?page=all (20.07.2008)

topics that in this case are for instance the doubt or self-doubts, the fact of loving women he cannot reach and the preference for progressive topics that were part of some of his movies, too. After his other collections of short stories, in "Mere Anarchy" Woody Allen again shows his satirical attitude and his special way of humor. Just reading the titles of the short stories, one can guess that while reading the stories, there will more behind them than one expected to be. In "Mere Anarchy" Allen further depicts situations out of the protagonist's lives that are at the same time absurd, somehow ordinary but nevertheless exceptional. Considering that in *Surprise Rocks Disney Trial*, Mickey Mouse has to witness against the Disney corporate group during a lawsuit or that in *Sam, You Made The Pants Too Fragrant*, there is a man who gets into intensive care because he got an electrical shot from a suit, it is obvious that Woody Allen holds his popular line of satirical and extraordinary way of writing. So, his classic attitude and quality remains for the typical Allen reader. Nevertheless, it is somehow like with his movies, there are some stories that one may like or dislike; everyone has to choose the fitting story or movie on his own.

Sam, You Made The Pants Too Fragrant is the story that will be relevant for this paper. In our expert session we discussed the problem, why especially this story was chosen to be discussed in class. Some reactions of the students contained that in this story Allen depicts his characteristic of old fashioned humor, as there are references to S.J. Perelman and the Marx Brothers (name of the protagonist: "Duckworth" → "Ducksauce/Duckbill/Ducksoup") and that he again illustrates his attitude towards progress and technology as he already has done in his 1971 movie *Bananas*. Introducing, this paper will give a short outline of the short story and then concentrate on special issues within the story by analyzing it and giving a possible background for the short story. Furthermore the reactions from our expert session in class and Woody Allen's position towards progress in life will be discussed in the conclusion part.

1. "SAM, YOU MADE THE PANTS TOO FRAGRANT"

1.1 THE STORY

Sam, You Made The Pants Too Fragrant is the third story from Woody Allen's short story collection "Mere Anarchy" from 2007. The short story is based on the article "The Year in Ideas: Enhanced Clothing", by Gina Bellafante, from *The New York Times Magazine*, from December 15, 2002[4]. Besides *Sam, You Made The Pants Too Fragrant*, there are other short stories in this book which are also catalyzed from newspaper or magazine articles that are based on real events. So, the short story is introduced by this article which discusses the phenomenon of "Technologically Enabled Clothing"[5]. Out of the article's topic, this short story developed and Woody Allen worked in some of the real facts that are mentioned in the article. That is for instance the fabric that can imprison different scents, in order to smell good all the time or shirts that can recharge cell-phones. In the following, first the story will be summarized, later a possible background and a further analysis will follow.

1.1.1 A SUMMARY OF THE PLOT

Benno Duckworth, the protagonist of the story, is a simple and undemanding man who writes articles about anapestic dimeter. One day, by accident, Duckworth meets his old friend Reg Millipede. They have a kind of superficial conversation – especially caused from Millipede's side – about technological clothing. Duckworth notices a spout, hidden under Millipede's lapel, from where he seems to drink something. He asks Millipede about the meaning of this specialty and he starts to inform Duckworth about his extraordinary suit that contains a "built-in hydration system"[6], a tank and a computer that is connected to a pump which functions as some kind of pipeline for his drinks. Millipede recommends and advises Duckworth to visit the special tailoring establishment of "Bandersnatch and Bushelman" on Savile Row, in order to buy some new clothes and to do up his outer appearance.

---

[4] Comp.: ALLEN, Woody: Mere Anarchy. UK: Ebury Press/Random House Group Company, 2007.
[5] ALLEN, Woody: Mere Anarchy. p. 25.
[6] ALLEN, Woody: Mere Anarchy. p. 25.

Duckworth does so and one day visits "Bandersnatch and Bushelman". Arriving at the shop, first he is treated as if he was at the wrong place. He has to defend himself in front of the salesman Binky Peplum and explain that he is a normal customer who comes on recommendation of Reg Millipede. Peplum starts to find out what Duckworth is looking for and gives him to understand that his current outer appearance and style is everything but en vogue. While Duckworth is looking for a simple and classic three-button to be worn on special occasions, Peplum tries to convince him of several novelties in the field of fashion and style. He mentions suits that imprison the aroma of freshly baked rolls or the scent of flowers or suits that reject any odor and again other suits that are made of a special fabric which is dirt resistant or providing a good mood.

Both have discussion on several suits with technological and – for Duckworth completely unknown – new features. Although Benno Duckworth seems to be interested in these special garments, he cannot get out of his old standard and resists in his opinion of having a simple but elegant blue suit. Just at the point of getting fed up with the situation and nearly taking out the pepper spray of his pocket, Duckworth himself notices a suit, which Peplum up to that point did not mention. It is a suit that can recharge cell-phone by rubbing the phone on the sleeves of the suit. Duckworth likes the idea of having a suit that is both practical but also matching with his ideas of a regular suit. While he seems to having made his choice, the other salesman, Ramsbottom, comes in to inform Peplum about an incidence referring another customer who also bought the cellular recharging suit. While Peplum tries to give Ramsbottom a hint not to go too deep into the topic, Ramsbottom explains that a customer who bought exact the same suit one day ago, now is in intensive care because he got an electrical shot after getting into contact with metal while wearing the suit. While Peplum remarks that this is the fourth time that a customer makes such an experience, he notices that Duckworth has disappeared. He himself decided that it is the best to go and find a regular three-button suit at Barneys, without any technological or postmodern features.

1.1.2 A POSSIBLE BACKGROUND OF THE STORY

"Sam, You Made The Pants Too Long"

Trousers dragging, slowly dragging through the street

Yes! I'm walking, but I'm walking without feet!

I'm not finding fault at all

You're too big and I'm too small

But Sam, you promised me both ends would meet

You made the coat and vest fit the best

You made the lining nice and strong

But Sam, you made the pants too long

You made the peak lapel look so swell

So who am I to say you're wrong?

But Sam, you made the pants too long

They got a belt and they got suspenders

So what can they lose?

But what good are belts and suspenders

When the pants are hanging over the shoes

You feel a winter breeze up and down the knees

The belt is where the tie belongs

'Cause Sam, Sam, Sam you made the pants too long!

During our research for the expert session and the topic of Woody Allen`s *Sam, You Made The Pants Too Fragrant*, we came across with the 30s song *Sam, You Made the Pants Too Long*. The song was popularized in 1932 by the comedian and singer Joe E. Lewis. Later it became more familiar to audiences through Barbara Streisand and The Supremes.

The *Sam* in the title and in the lyrics is not clearly identified but the assumption that it may refer to the Jewish tailor Samuel Beckenstein, is not far fetched. This can be guessed due to the fact that the Social Security Death Index records give the evidence that a Samuel Beckenstein has lived from 1893-1968. He owned a tailor shop in New York City, whereas New York is not directly mentioned in the song. But nevertheless, it spreads the mood and the ambiance of the Jewish Lower East Side in New York City, where Samuel Beckenstein got his clothing store on 130 Orchard Street[7]. In correspondence to the short story it should be stress at this point that it is not exactly mentioned that the protagonist or the other characters within the story are Jewish. One can just assume – with reference to the fact that Woody Allen is Jewish and that most of his characters in his movies are Jews – that within the story at least Benno Duckworth maybe Jewish. While talking about Jewishness, as mentioned above, Barbara Streisand is one of the artists who also performed this song. Considering that she herself is Jewish and that she is one of the greatest icons for Jews, with this a further link between song and story is given.

---

[7] Comp.:http://www.barrypopik.com/index.php/new_york_city/entry/sam_you_made_the_pants_too_long_1932/ (20.07.2008)

But besides the fact of Jewishness and the enormously similar title of the song and the short story, there is another fundamental connection between both of them. As the lyrics above illustrate, the topic of the song corresponds to the basic theme of the short story, namely clothes and fabrics. But while the song is based on the traditional work of a tailor and his fabrics, the story deals with the up-to-date topic of technological clothing, progress in fashion and its "pitfalls". Furthermore there is the fact that Woody Allen is famous for the use of songs from the 1930s in his movies, what for instance comes through in *Everyone Says I Love You*. So, why he should not use a song from the 30s as the basis for a short story, which is made up on the same topic as the song?

According to these correspondences and connections, the assumption that the song may have been a basis for Woody Allen`s *Sam, You Made The Pants Too Fragrant*, should not be too far fetched. Nevertheless, there has not been an exactly explanation that or evident reference that Allen`s short story is really based on this song; it is just a matching example.

1.2 ANALYZING THE STORY

Going over to the analysis of *Sam, You Made The Pants Too Fragrant*, it is to mention, that first only a short excerpt will be analyzed in detail, while the further explanations will refer to the whole short story.

In order to analyze a certain excerpt from the story, I have chosen a section, where the protagonist`s attitude and his perception towards the technological clothing starts to change. So, it is some kind of transition from his old standards to a newer one but nevertheless not long lasting. The passage starts at the top of page 32 and goes up to the bottom of the same page: "'Well, it`s motivated by the suit. [...]' [...] 'Now, that`s more like it,' [...]". This excerpt is situated in a part, where Benno Duckworth by some means stands between his traditional opinion of clothes and the suit he is looking for and the change of his view towards the postmodern fashion. While in the earlier parts and in the beginning of this excerpt he is somehow confused about the new way of garments and wonders what it is good for, in the end of this passage he seems to change his mind according this topic.

The setting of this passage is the tailoring establishment "Bandersnatch and Bushelman" where postmodern fabrics and clothes are sold. There are two characters, Benno Duckworth – the protagonist of the short story – and Binky Peplum, the salesman; both of them also appear before and after this selected passage. From the beginning of the story, the protagonist is by

8

some means presented as the typical Woody Allen character; or better said, one directly gets the impression that this is a character, which Woody Allen himself could act out in one of his movies. This happens due to the fact that Duckworth fulfills the typical "Allen stereotypes" such as the nervous and neurotic personality, the problem of anxiety and uneasiness or the aspect that he, as the protagonist, gets humiliated by the other characters, as they judge about his outer appearance[8] or for instance his wife[9]. Duckworth seems to be a defensive person, who basically wants to try out something new but he is not really sure about it and he cannot really get out of his old standards. Whereas Binky Peplum gives the impression of being an offensive character, who is open minded and talks straight out what he thinks. Therefore he also appears some kind of insulting or "know-it-all" when he tries to sell Duckworth the postmodern fashion.

As this passage is part of a short story, which goes over circa 10 pages, this part is embedded into – or better said framed by – the whole plot. The same as it is during the whole story, this passage too is dominated by the dialogue between the salesman and Benno Duckworth. So, out of their talks – which form the main part of the story – and the stream of consciousness of the narrator, the reader can make out their minds and understand their positions. Furthermore considering that both are standing within in the shop, this situation may be extremely uncomfortable for Duckworth because he is treated in an annoying way. This feeling especially comes through, when the reader can follow Duckworth` thoughts. He, as the narrator of the story, gives information about his inner feelings and his perception of the circumstances he is in. The sentence "As the fingers in my pocket closed around my pepper spray should any attempt to hamper egress be made, [...]"[10] taken out from the chosen passage, depicts very well that Duckworth seems to be the nervous character who feels uneasy and uncomfortable because of the salesman`s pressure.

As already mentioned above, this passage is framed by the rest of the short story; it is embedded in the whole progress and development of the events. From the moment when Duckworth steps into the tailoring establishment, Peplum is trying to sell him one of the postmodern suits, while Duckworth basically is not really interested in them. At the same time, Peplum does not leave out to offend Duckworth personally.

After some hopeless tries, in this passage again, Peplum tries to convince his old fashioned customer about the technological and useful clothing. But despite his anxious and nervous

---

[8] ALLEN, Woody: Mere Anarchy. p. 27
[9] ALLEN, Woody: Mere Anarchy. p. 30
[10] ALLEN, Woody: Mere Anarchy. p. 32

personality, Duckworth finds a fault or better said a gap in the system of the postmodern garments. While in the beginning Duckworth makes way for Peplum's verbal "attacks" by reacting friendly and calm but nevertheless tensed and nervous (e.g. p. 28: passage with aromas; p. 30: passage with fabric that can reject any odor), in this passage he begins to question the things that are presented to him. When Peplum tries to convince Duckworth about another suit that can provide a constant mood of well-being and let's the wearer forget all his problems, Duckworth questions the point that one would experience withdrawal symptoms when taking off the suit made of "antidepressant textiles" (p. 32: "but when I take off the suit […]"). As a result to this Peplum reacts some kind of irritated (p. 32: "Er, well, there are some weak sister […]") but with his question in return ("Would you ever contemplate ending it all?") however, he shows how sure he is about the postmodern clothing and its advantages. With this he somehow frightens Duckworth in such a way that he feels the need of reaching for his pepper spray that is in his pocket and inventing a white lie about a pet raccoon in order to leave the shop. Just in this moment, without any support from Peplum, Duckworth himself observes a suit that arouses his interest ("[…] my attention was caught by a stunning navy swatch […]"). So he asks for it and Peplum again does his job and praises the clothing, which this time is a suit that recharges cell-phones by rubbing the phone on the sleeves. The fact that Duckworth himself gets interested in one of the garments is a turning point in this short story. While in the beginning and in the whole course of the story Peplum tries to persuade and convince Duckworth about the postmodern clothing, now he is the one who searches for information in order to be up to date according this suit. Another difference is that Duckworth is really interested in the suit ("Now, that's more like it"), what shows that although he had his traditional view towards these garments and that he reacted kind of paranoid towards theses novelties, he is able to change his mind, as long as he is confronted with something that is useful and appropriate to his expectations (pp. 32/33"[…] envisioning the finished product to be at once stylish yet practical […]"). With this change of mind, the reader is confronted with an unexpected situation in this moment of transition what has the effect that the interest for the rest of the story raises.

Furthermore this passage, and the short story as a whole, is striking referring the choice of words Allen uses. As it became typical for him in his prose, he uses unusual words for normal things, so that from time to time the reader has problems in understanding what was really meant. Of course this demands some special knowledge of the Allen language or his special style and references he may make; but nevertheless it is somehow surprising to come across with words like kumquat, egress or horrendous, when the reader is not confronted with them in his/her daily life.

As a whole this passage seems to fit perfectly into the flow of the short story, as it first describes a turning point which the protagonist experiences. But considering that in the end of the story the Duckworth again changes his mind after having heard that another customer is in intensive care because he wore the rechargeable suit and got an electrical shock, the reader again is confronted with an unexpected situation: "High voltage in a pair of pants […] sends me ricocheting directly to Barneys, where I bought a marked-down three-button job […]" (p. 34). Duckworth leaves the store without buying anything and this shows how surprising things can develop and that he again drops into his old standards trying to flee from the postmodern and brand new vogue.

2. CONCLUSION: WOODY ALLEN AND PROGRESS IN LIFE

In his short story compilation "Mere Anarchy" Woody Allen depicts stories, which mostly have in common that the protagonist has to experience some new form of humiliation or suffering, in order to be up-to-date and to go with the brand new vogue and fashion. This is also given in this story discussed above. As it is typical of Woody Allen the reader can find some of his trademarks while reading the stories; so it is of course in *Sam, You Made The Pants Too Fragrant*.

This leads over to the question, in how far this chosen short story depicts the typical "allenesque elements" or rather in how far this is a typical Woody Allen story? Besides the classic facts that we have a protagonist who is nervous, neurotic and quiet paranoid when he is confronted with something new, our expert-session according this topic brought about some other points. We found out, that further typical Allen elements like the anxiety problems of the protagonist – which especially come through when following his thoughts – the absurd and grotesque way of acting and the all in all somehow absurd but nevertheless realistic topic of the short story are proof enough that this is a typical Woody Allen story. Nevertheless some students argued that the story would not offer enough capacity to make a movie out of it. Of course there are these characteristic elements that are also common in his movies but besides the fact that it is a *short* story, the plot as a whole would have to be extended in order to fill a movie with it; although the topic chosen for the story is an up-to-date subject, as the current fashion world shows (e.g. Hussein Chalayan and his collection of technological clothing that transforms and morphs).

Concentrating on the topic of the story, it comes up the question, how *Sam, You Made The Pants Too Fragrant* depicts technology in life. Reactions during the expert session showed that it is portrayed as a threat to humans and that people are unconsciously forced to purchase these things because the industry makes them think that they need these things. Of course other reactions also contained that technology or rather technological garments can have their advantages, as they may have several functions so that one is always suitable dressed for two or more occasions, for instance. Furthermore they can be helpful with regard to medical issues or for the space flight: considering that the garments have some special features that enable people to do things they are not able to do in certain circumstances, it gets evident that these clothes can have a useful effect. Yet the story shows the pitfalls of all these technological and progressive novelties and that they can change ones life in an unexpected and harmful way. So, technology is represented as an issue that is a "must-have", which in fact is only useless luxury and therefore not really necessary.

This is also portrayed in Woody Allen`s 1971 movie *Bananas* where the protagonist works for a company that invents office furniture with technological features, in order to save time and bring forward the aspect of multi-tasking: the office chair is transformed into a bike, the telephones function as dumbbells and out of the file drawer a basketball appears. But here too, we can first see how good technology can function in our daily life, that it has its advantages and that it can make our lives easier. But here again the protagonist gets inferior to this progress of technology as the postmodern office furniture does not function any more in the right way. The movie, as the short story, presents how important time-management becomes in life of humankind and questions where civilization is moving.

Considering that Woody Allen depicted this topic 26 years ago in one of his movies and now again exclusively concentrates on it in a short story gives the evidence, that Allen has a certain relation to this subject. Furthermore today the topic of technology is more a part of our lives than it was during the 1970s; therefore Woody Allen illustrates a quiet contemporary and existing topic in his story, what of course arouses the question about his personal attitude towards this theme. Can one say that he still is or ever was modern or *en vogue*? Allen of course holds his line by working with his old fashioned humor and the well-known references he makes, for instance concerning the Marx Brothers or Perelman. He depicts current topics like technology and progress in life but nevertheless he regards them critical and with a sharp wit and observation of contemporary life.

Talking about the story as a whole and about its topic, it comes out that this story also has its meaning and a certain message that Allen tries to transmit – as he does in all of his works. Technology of course can be useful and people can experience its advantages in life, but *Sam, You Made The Pants Too Fragrant* furthermore depicts that people should not always accept everything what the consumer society offers, without questioning it in advance. Allen somehow presents a denial of postmodernism and the fast progress of technology in our lives, as he portrays the new inventions as malicious and even dangerous. Technology in the field of clothing and fashion is described as something unnecessary and as something that may exists too much in our present-day's society, the same as it exists *too* much of everything. Furthermore Allen may wanted to stress that people should accept and get along with the old and traditional conventions to which all people are used to. So, he illustrates technology as something useful but at the same time as something that can hold dangers of abuse when used by the wrong people or in the wrong circumstances and that it has its pitfalls according its function and application.

3. BIBLIOGRAPHY

➢ ALLEN, Woody: Mere Anarchy. UK: Ebury Press/Random House Group Company, 2007.

➢ FUCHS, Wolfgang J.: Die vielen Gesichter des Woody Allen. Köln: Benedikt Taschen Verlag, 1986.

➢ YACOWAR, Maurice: Loser Take All. The Comic Art of Woody Allen. USA: Frederick Ungar Publishing Co., Inc., 1979.

Internet resources:

➢ https://www.commentarymagazine.com/viewarticle.cfm/mere-anarchy-by-woody-allen-10944?page=all (20.07.2008)

➢ http://www.barrypopik.com/index.php/new_york_city/entry/sam_you_made_the_pants_too_long_1932/ (20.07.2008)